Oxford Prima

A Family
First World War

Valerie Fawcett

**Katy finds
out about her
great grandmother**

Oxford University Press 1993

What was life like before the First World War?
Katy's great grandmother was a maid in a big house.
She was called Ada, and she worked very hard.

In the morning, she cleaned out the fireplaces in all the rooms.
There was no central heating.
She polished the fire grates and put in fresh coal.
Then she carried hot water to the bedrooms for the family to wash.

While Ada made the fires, another maid did the family washing.
She put the sheets and towels in a tank called a copper. A fire under the copper heated the water and the maid stirred the clothes to get them clean.

Then she rinsed them in clean water in a bath.
She had to put them through a mangle to squeeze out the water.
There were no washing machines to make washing easy.

After breakfast, Ada had to clean the rooms.
She spread wet tea leaves on the floors to catch the dust.
Then she swept the floors with a broom.
There were very few vacuum cleaners.
After that, she made the beds.

In the afternoon Ada cleaned the brass and silver dishes.
After tea, she lit the fires in the bedrooms.
It was a long day.
In the winter she made the beds warm with a special
pan filled with hot coals.

Ada had one day off each week.
Sometimes she met her boyfriend, Thomas, in the park. They listened to the women who wanted to be able to vote in elections.

Women were not allowed to vote in 1910.
Ada and other men and women thought they should be.
The women who went on marches to ask for the vote were called the Suffragettes.

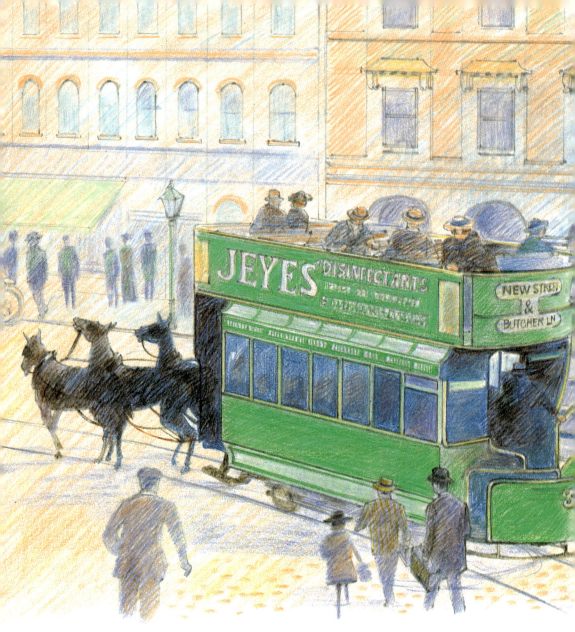

Thomas was a tram driver.
The trams ran along rails in the road.
Most people travelled on trams and steam trains.
There were not many buses like we have today.

There were very few cars and they were very expensive.
They often broke down.
Most rich people still had carriages which were pulled by horses.
Horses pulled taxis, vans and fire engines too.

Ada and Thomas sometimes went to the music hall.
The music hall was a theatre but they did not see a play.
They saw singers and dancers and jugglers.

Sometimes the audience joined in the singing.
There were very few cinemas before the First World War.
People had only just started to make films.

In 1914, the First World War started.
It was called a World War because so many countries took part.
Soldiers from Britain went to fight German soldiers in France.

Thomas became a soldier.
Ada went to see him off at the station.
The train had a coal fire in the engine which turned water into steam.
The power from the steam made the wheels go round.

15

When the war started, life in Britain went on as before. But the German navy attacked the ships bringing food to Britain.
By 1917 there was not enough food in the shops.

People were given ration books.
They had to give the coupons to the shopkeepers when they bought food.
Everyone had to have a fair share.
It was a special day when a shop had oranges to sell.

There was no television or radio at this time. People found out what was happening by reading newspapers and posters.
Many people bought a newspaper in the morning and another in the evening.

Soldiers told their families and friends about the war in their letters.
People in Britain did not hear news from far-away countries until a long time after it happened.

In 1918, the war ended.
A lot of people had died in the war.
A lot of people also died after the war from an illness called influenza.
Today, it is not a bad illness, but in 1919 there were no medicines to kill the infections.

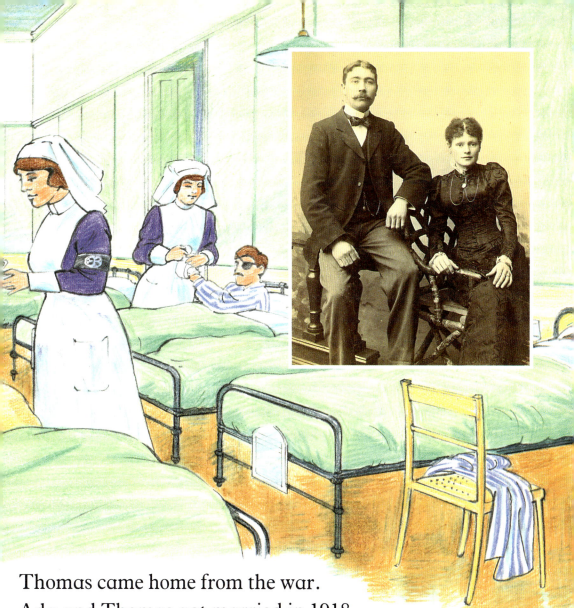

Thomas came home from the war.
Ada and Thomas got married in 1918.
Ada had to leave her job because she was married.
People did not like having married servants.
Thomas became a tram driver again.
They were happy that the war was over.

Katy's Family Tree

Ada, born in 1890
Katy's Great Gran

Thomas, born in 1890
Katy's Great Grandad

married in 1918

Charles, born in 1919

Jean, born in 1920
Katy's Gran

Irene, born in 1921

Dorothy, born in 1923

Will, born in 1930

George, born in 1919, **Katy's** Grandad

married in 1946

Martin, born in 1953
Katy's Dad

Susan, born in 1953
Katy's Mum

John, born in 1946
Katy's Uncle

married in 1975

Katy, born in 1986

Tom, born in 1978

Prices

d = old penny   s = shilling

3d (1¼p)

2d (¾p)

3d (1¼p)

£200

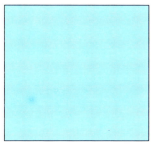
Radio not invented

Television not invented

How much did people earn each week?

Engine driver £2 0s 6d (£2.02p)

Factory worker £1 10s 1d (£1.50p)

Index

bedroom 3, 7
bread 23
buses 10
carriages 11
cars 11, 23
cinemas 13
cleaning 6–7
coal 3, 7
copper 4
engine 15
films 13
fire engines 11
fireplaces 3
fires 3, 4, 7, 15
First World War 2, 13, 14
food 16, 17, 23
health 20–21
heating 3
horses 11
houses and homes 2, 3
illness 20
influenza 20
kitchen 4–5
living room 2–3, 6
maid 2, 4
mangle 5

marriage 21
medicines 20
milk 23
music hall 12
newspapers 18
potatoes 23
radio 18, 23
ration books 17
servants 21
ships 16
shopping 16–17
soldiers 14, 15, 18, 19
station 14–15
steam trains 10, 15
streets 10–11, 18–19
Suffragettes 9
taxis 11
television 18, 23
trams 10, 21
transport 10–11, 15
vacuum cleaner 6
vans 11
votes 8, 9
washing 3, 4
washing machine 5
water 3, 5, 15
women 8, 9

Acknowledgements
Illustrations: Barry Rowe (main pictures and cover), and Lynne Willey (family tree, title page and back cover).
Photos: Tony Dale p 21; Imperial War Museum p 17; Rob Judges (front cover, title page and back cover).

Oxford University Press, Walton Street,
Oxford, OX2 6DP
© Oxford University Press 1993
ISBN 0 19 917173 4
Phototypeset by Pentacor, High Wycombe, Bucks
Printed in Hong Kong